THE
CONFESSIONS
OF
CONGRESSMAN X

THE
CONFESSIONS
★ ★ ★ OF ★ ★ ★
CONGRESSMAN X

*A disturbing and shockingly frank tell-all
of vanity, greed and deceit*

CONGRESSMAN X

Mill City Press, Minneapolis

Mill City Press, Inc.
322 First Avenue N, 5th floor
Minneapolis, MN 55401
612.455.2293
www.millcitypublishing.com

The photo on the cover is a professional model. His resemblance to any current or former member of Congress is entirely coincidental.

ISBN-13: 978-1-63413-973-1
LCCN: 2016904904

Cover Design by Alan Pranke
Typeset by MK Ross

Printed in the United States of America

CONTENTS

FOREWORD: WHO IS CONGRESSMAN X?

★ ★ ★

I first met Congressman X at a dinner party in Washington, but I won't reveal the year, as it would narrow down his identity. For reasons I shall explain, X wishes to forever remain anonymous.

At the time of our encounter and until 2007, I was the editor of *Hideaway Report*, a luxury travel newsletter I founded in 1979 under the nom de plume Andrew Harper. Respected for its candid and authentic reviews of intimate worldwide hotels and resorts, the publication has been featured in the *New York Times*, *Wall Street Journal*,

USA Today, *Forbes*, *National Geographic Traveler*, and more.

Most of my readers were celebrities, CEOs, and presidents of companies seeking peaceful and unspoiled places far from the madding crowd. A dozen members of Congress were also subscribers, including affable Congressman X. We instantly hit it off because of his love of travel and because I was a political junkie, having been the chief of staff and press secretary for two House members in the 1970s.

We eventually became friends and confidants and met once or twice a year, usually when I stopped in Washington for an overnight following one of my exploratory trips around the world. I would share with him my travel adventures and hotel discoveries, and he would reciprocate with the latest Capitol Hill insider information. We felt very much at ease with each other and knew our conversations would never go further than the restaurant booth where we sat. As the years passed, our talks became darker as X shared his remarkably frank observations of Congress. Many of his revelations were unsettling to me, and I began jotting them down from memory immediately after our get-togethers. I thought he might want to publish them in a tell-all book after he left Congress.

We continued to see each other after I retired. It was on one of those occasions that I told him about my notes and gave him a copy. He was initially outraged and felt I had betrayed his confidences and our friendship. I assured him I never discussed our conversations with anyone and would never do so without his consent. This seemed to please him, though he refused to talk to me for eight months.

One day, out of the blue, he phoned and said he wanted to see me about a private matter. I detected a sense of urgency in his voice and agreed to fly to Washington the following week. We met in my hotel suite. Following small talk, he suddenly asked if I still had the raw transcripts of our earlier conversations. I told him I did and that I had not shared them with anyone, as promised. He clapped me on the shoulder, obviously pleased with my answer.

"I read the copy you gave me several times and must say you accurately quoted me," X said. "I wish I had the balls to speak out publicly about the sad state of affairs in this town as I did with you. Brutal stuff. Unfortunately, I don't have the fortitude or desire to soil my legacy. I also don't want to embarrass my family or the congressional colleagues I've worked with through the years. Nor do I want to subject myself to a barrage of incoming crap from the hard-nosed progressives in my party.

"That said, I'm wondering if you'd be interested in publishing my manifesto sometime in the future? You have a solid reputation for confidentiality, and I trust you. But you'd have to keep my identity a secret and not provide any hints that might lead one to figure out who I am."

I told him I would be pleased to edit such a book but that it would be more compelling and persuasive if his name were mentioned. He would have none of it and made me swear I would never reveal his identity. In the end, I agreed to oversee his book because I believe his disturbing observations need to be urgently debated by the American people.

I met with Congressman X on two subsequent occasions. At both meetings, he made some minor alterations to the transcripts to clarify his commentary and update some factual data. We never talked again until he recently gave me the go-ahead to publish his forthright opinions. I asked the reason for his sudden decision and he cited the public's "surprisingly boisterous disdain with Washington" that's bubbled forth during the 2016 presidential campaign.

His "confessions" are in his own words, unimpeded by the intrusion of my cross-questions or other verbal exchanges. For ease of reading, I have taken the liberty of organizing his rambling thoughts into separate chapters based on the subjects he addressed over the years. As a result, this slim volume is not a narrative but rather a collection of his provocative remarks.

At my insistence, I wrote this introduction that X agreed not to review prior to publication. He also gave me carte blanche to oversee the copy and design of the front and back covers, which I "sensationalized" to create a heightened curiosity in the book. He will undoubtedly be furious with my latter efforts, though he clearly understands it takes a bit of melodrama these days to engage the attention of the electorate.

In keeping with our confidentiality pact, I have gone out of my way to protect his identity by redacting certain names and dates he referred to. I also won't reveal whether X retired, lost reelection, or is still serving in Congress. I can report he's a Democrat (which becomes self-evident in his comments), though his remarks are representative of many Republicans as well. Human nature being what it is, there will be some who will fervently try to identify X, perhaps for retribution. Trust me, it's a hopeless task, for even I was fooled by his duplicitous persona.

The sophisticated reader will realize most of Congressman X's revelations are not new and have been parsed over in the press for years. The difference is the shockingly frank and outrageous manner in which he condemns Congress and the electorate. Indeed, it is easy to understand his insistence on anonymity, for he paints an alarming picture of a dysfunctional institution dominated by a coterie of deceitful career politicians who revel in the power they possess and the special-interest money that's lavished upon them. As X so eloquently puts it: "I've come to the conclusion the whole Washington scene represents a diminishment of civilization. Our country's in a free-fall to mediocrity, and Congress is leading the way."

Many will be appalled by Congressman X's arrogant attitude, particularly his lack of remorse for deluding and mocking those he was elected to serve. He may be fed up with a legislative system that has run amok, but he places much of the blame for that outcome on an apathetic and gullible public who feels powerless about changing the status quo. X once told me he wanted his revelations to "make people's blood boil." Indeed, X's audacity conjures up fictional TV newsman Howard Beale, who pleaded with his listeners to open their windows and yell, 'I'm as mad as hell, and I'm not going to take this anymore!' But as X points out in the final chapter, most of us will probably keep our windows shut and watch out for our own self-interest.

Robert Atkinson
February 2016

The Confessions of Congressman X
in His Own Words . . .

VOTERS ARE INCREDIBLY IGNORANT

★ ★ ★

. . . and know little about our form of government and how it works. Ask them to name the three branches of government, and they're clueless. The Chief Justice of the Supreme Court. Forget it. Hell, I'm lucky if my constituents know my name and what I do. What was it Churchill said? 'The best argument against democracy is a brief chat with the average voter.'

I once asked a fellow about the content of the Constitution. 'It gives me the right to own a gun,' he replied. 'What else?' I asked. 'That's pretty much it.' So there you have it. Another knucklehead with the right to vote.

It's difficult to maintain a well-functioning democracy if the electorate doesn't possess a modicum of proficiency in civics. Or doesn't take the time or have any interest to follow what's going on in Washington. How stupid is that? Apathy encourages politicians to pull wool over the eyes of constituents. To engage in publicity stunts. To trade votes for campaign contributions.

Perception is reality, and reality is whatever I decide it to be. On controversial bills I sometimes vote 'yes' on a motion and 'no' on an amendment so I can claim I'm on either side of an issue. It's the old shell game: if you can't convince 'em, confuse 'em. Welcome to the congressional fantasyland of sound bites and slogans, where form prevails over substance, and no one really knows what the hell's true and what's false.

I contradict myself all the time, but few people notice. One minute I rail against excessive spending and ballooning debt. The next minute I'm demanding more spending on education, health care, unemployment benefits, conservation projects, yadda yadda yadda. I'm for having everything, just like my constituents.

Voters claim they want substance and detailed position papers, but what they really crave are cutesy cat videos, celebrity gossip, top 10 lists, reality TV shows, tabloid tripe, and the next fucking Twitter message.

We've become a superficial nation obsessed with fluff. Americans may be hard-pressed to name their two senators or find Afghanistan on a map, but they know everything about the loopy Kardackians [sic] and Brad and what's-her-name. I worry about our country's future when critical issues take a backseat to the inane utterings of illiterate athletes and celebrity twits.

Voters claim they're too busy to keep up with what's going on in Washington. Like being busy were some kind of modern-day affliction. Fact is, a lot of these folks are too busy watching out for themselves—crafting their fictional brand on Facebook, YouTube, and Instagram. All the world's a stage, and they want to be the star. I know, I know, we're no different than the narcissists we represent: We're out for ourselves, we lie when necessary, and money is everything. [*Laughs*]. There's no business like show business.

It's far easier than you think to manipulate a nation of naïve, self-absorbed sheep who crave instant gratification.

Things are so partisan today most folks vote the straight party line, even though they don't know shit about who they're voting for. They just don't want the other guys to win.

I HAD HIGH HOPES WHEN I WAS FIRST ELECTED TO CONGRESS

★ ★ ★

. . . and was pretty naïve. I quickly found out devotion to party, PAC loyalty, and getting reelected were the main orders of business.

Politics is all the same. The party caucus rules, and the Speaker holds all the cards. To get along you have to go along. Grow old, hold your tongue, vote the party line, and one day maybe you'll get a key committee assignment or chair a subcommittee. In the meantime, pay attention to the needs of your big donors.

I always wanted to be a senator, but it never worked out. What a life those stuffed pigeons have. Six years pretending to be statesmen. No wonder they thumb their noses at us sorry House asses perpetually running for reelection. Begging for bucks 24/7.

It didn't take me long to grasp how badly our legislative process is broken. And no one seems to give a damn. We spend money we don't have and blithely mortgage the future with a wink and a nod. Everything's for the here and now. Screw the next generation.

When I first arrived in Washington, the extent of anger and partisanship really stunned me. Not just in Congress. Every government department, agency, and regulatory board seems politicized. Even 'impartial' judges seem to toc the party line when it comes to adjudicating political matters for those who appointed them. It's scary when you think about it.

There doesn't seem to be any sense of order or decorum in Congress. There certainly isn't any bipartisan deliberation. No thoughtful exchange of ideas. Everything is confrontational and done for the benefit of one's party. It's my way or the highway. The common good is rarely a consideration.

This town's a sinkhole of leeches. Everyone's trying to manipulate the political system to his own special advantage, often to the detriment of the country.

How ironic we've become a bunch of out-of-touch insiders. Everyone bitches but most of us are easily reelected because the polarized public's scared to death of the other party.

It used to be that character counted. That voters took into account honesty and integrity before pulling the lever. Now it's all about who shares your views and will look after your interests. Ethics aren't a big concern of voters. They just want you to give them what they want.

Like most of my colleagues, I promise my constituents a lot of stuff I can never deliver. But what the hell? If it makes them happy hearing it, and they're stupid enough to believe it, shame on them.

Forget public service. We all come here with good intentions, but as time passes, it becomes all about self-service and selfish survival.

Pogo was right: We've seen the enemy, and he is us.

MY MAIN JOB IS TO KEEP MY JOB

★　★　★

. . . to get reelected. It takes precedence over everything. I know that sounds crass, but it's just the way it is. My colleagues are no different. We all spend an obscene amount of time dialing for dollars when we ought to be legislating and getting to know each other.

If Mr. Smith went to Washington today, he'd be like the rest of us. His every move calculated on raising money and getting reelected.

I'd rather have a colonoscopy than ask people for money. I hate feeling beholden to someone or some group. I hate attending fundraisers where I feel like a puppet performing for those who enrich me. It's not why I came to Washington, but it's the reality of the job.

Fundraising is so time-consuming I seldom read any bills I vote on. I don't even know how they'll be implemented or what they'll cost. My staff gives me a last-minute briefing before I go to the floor and tells me whether to vote yea or nay. How bad is that?

You know why I want to keep my seat? I like the power and recognition. The opportunity to be at the center of things. To make my mark on history and mold the society in which I live.

Getting reelected requires the old give and take. First, you have to give away taxpayer monies to provide legislative favors, tax breaks, and subsidies to constituents and special-interest groups. You then take some back in the form of donations from those to whom you've provided such favors, tax breaks, and subsidies. Ain't democracy beautiful?

Every lawmaker talks about the need to simplify the tax code, but we don't mean it. Targeted tax breaks, loopholes, deductions, credits, deferments, write-offs, incentives, subsidies. Hell, these are some of the best ways we have to dole out favors to contributors.

We only kid ourselves when we say political donations have no effect on our voting. Folks know we're disingenuous. But damn it, we need all the financial support we can muster to fund today's hugely expensive reelection campaigns.

Nowadays, it costs about $2.5 million to win a seat in the House. Real competitive races can be much more. That's a lot of

money to raise. Thankfully, it's much easier
for me now that I have some seniority
under my belt and serve on the [*name
of committee deleted*]. A lot of donations
come my way without having to ask. I
suppose some donors view it as a form of
protection payment, since they know I can
influence the tone of legislation before the
committee. That's not the case, however.

Sure, during hearings I sometimes lob
softball questions to witnesses from
industries that have contributed to my
campaign. No harm done. I view it
as a courtesy. I also occasionally offer
amendments provided me by special
interest supporters. Not an ideal situation,
I agree. But frankly, when we mark up the
language in most bills, my constituents
could care less about the nitty-gritty
details. Most don't even know what the
bill is about.

Can we make or break fortunes by adding seemingly innocuous riders to committee bills? You bet we can.

If a college student were to ask me how to prepare for Congress, I'd say, 'Major in marketing and finance so you can sell yourself to the electorate and requisite donors. A minor in theatre might also be helpful, so you can convince voters you're someone you're not.' [*Laughs.*]

FACTS, SCHMACTS. I'LL SAY ANYTHING TO GET ELECTED

★ ★ ★

. . . because most voters have short attention spans and won't remember a lot of what I said after Election Day. It's like a major sporting event. People remember who won, not how they got there.

No one's held accountable for campaign promises anymore. You can pretty much say what you want to get elected, and then do what you *really* want after you're elected.

Election campaigns are a pain in the ass. Unless I win. In which case it's a nice ego boost. Then it's back to shaking the money tree and selling access to me and my legislative staff.

I'd rather be crafting legislation in Washington than schmoozing with constituents at town hall meetings. Unfortunately, it's part of the game when you travel back home. Grip 'n' grin pictures, endless glad-handing and bullshitting with a lot of people your cat wouldn't drag home. Just shoot me. Why couldn't I have been elected for eternity?

Political consultants tell me to keep my message simple, vague, and forceful. Forget about engaging the intellect of the voters. Most are mentally lazy and bore easily. It's all about style, not substance. Memorable slogans, catchy metaphors, bite-size non-thoughts. Entertain their emotions and you'll win their hearts.

I've also learned it's important to cultivate a concocted image of myself. To make sure the public sees me as I want them to see me. Brand management 101. Shit, I'm marketed no differently than a fancy car or athletic shoes.

Image is everything. Charming liars get away with more than you know. Good looks and a Howdy Doody smile are always a plus.

During TV interviews I try to deliver forceful, clever power points, which my advisors try to pedal on YouTube. Who the hell watches YouTube?

I like to start my TV campaigns with feel-good ads centered on the simple lives of my parents and what they taught me in life. How I share the viewer's middle-class beliefs and dreams. How my upbringing has given me an understanding of their problems and what their lives are like. How they can count on me to fight for their interests. Hard to believe people still lap up such gauzy nonsense.

If I can dig up dirt on my opponent, all the better. Pollsters claim voters are turned off by negative advertising. Don't believe it. Attack ads work and help shape the opinions of swing voters, who decide most elections.

People see the world as they want to see the world. Facts be damned. Their crazy notions may not match reality, but if you want to be all things to all people—and get reelected—sometimes you just gotta climb down the rabbit hole and massage their egos. [*Laughs.*]

Few people give a crap about social issues on Election Day. The pocketbook always wins out.

How ironic that most of us in Congress run against Congress and the culture of corruption we perpetuate. It's as if we've all lost our fucking sanity and become Don Quixote setting our sights on righting all that's wrong in the political world we've created.

Insincerity from the heart. It's just another component of politics as usual.

SO MUCH OF WHAT I DO IS A FARCE— BULLSHIT RAISED TO AN ART FORM.

A lot of bills we consider are asinine. They do nothing but pander to special-interest groups or the folks back home. Nonbinding resolutions glorifying some fruit or vegetable. Bills designating National Heritage Months for every conceivable ethnic group. Naming bridges, buildings and streets after dearly departed colleagues. What a waste of time.

If you sat in the visitor's gallery, you'd observe nothing much happening. We give vanity speeches on the floor with few if any colleagues around. Inane blather to impress our constituents back home. Sometimes we become instant celebrities by booking a slot on C-SPAN to deliver a passionate prepared speech on some issue. According to protocol, the camera is focused directly on the speaker, so viewers never realize the chamber is empty.

I flatter constituents with birthday greetings on gold-embossed congressional stationary. Some folks proudly display them on their home or office walls. And they're over the moon when I commend them on achievements like a job promotion. Or cite their kid in the Congressional Record for making the honor roll. It's all a crock, but happy people mean more votes at the polls. And that's what it's all about.

A key part of my job is helping constituents cut through red tape and secure government benefits they feel are due them. Some try to game the system, but I don't care. When they come to me to ask for such favors, I feel like the Godfather. [*Laughs.*] Payback comes on Election Day when their gratitude translates into votes.

Nobody here gives a rat's ass about the future and who's going to pay for all this stuff we vote for. That's the next generation's problem. It's all about immediate publicity, getting credit now, lookin' good for the upcoming election.

You'd be amazed at the accounting gimmicks and voodoo legislative maneuvers we come up with to find fantasy savings to offset excess spending. Clamping down on government waste is always a favorite, along with supplemental spending bills not included in the official budget.

Both parties tend to avoid taking positions

on controversial matters like raising taxes or raising the retirement age for Social Security. Vote 'yes' on those kinds of issues, and come election time, your opponent runs ads reminding voters of your stupidity.

We also don't walk the talk when it comes to helping out small businesses. We may thump the podium for the little guy on Main Street, but most legislation favors the powerful corporations who donate to our campaign coffers.

Pat Moynihan once said Congress defined deviancy down from the standpoint of its behavior and lack of integrity. What he forgot to mention was the people we serve also don't live by their own ideals, except in their minds. [*Laughs.*]

DOES MONEY
CORRUPT?
OF COURSE IT DOES.

★ ★ ★

It certainly buys access and influence.
Oftentimes it sets the legislative agenda in
Congress.

Business organizations and unions fork
over more than $3 billion a year to those
who lobby the federal government. Does
that tell you something? We're operating a
fucking casino.

And don't forget those billionaire mega-
donors. One day a handful of the moneyed
few may actually control the whole election
process and reshape American policy to
their liking. It's already started to happen.

It's not just individual members of Congress the plutocrats, law firms, and lobbying conglomerates want to influence. It's entire committees and their staffs. They want to call the shots at the very point where legislation is written. To dictate the details of regulations that will benefit their clients.

It's not surprising some lawmakers and senior committee staff can be cooperative with lobbyists due to lucrative job possibilities. I know a few members who've already been offered a guaranteed future because of their name, connections, and knowledge of the inner workings of our complex legislative process.

Corruption and selfishness have always been part of the congressional process. It's human nature whenever you have special interests and money involved. It's not as bad as the early 1900s, but it's definitely a growing problem.

Does that mean the rich get richer and everyone else gets screwed? Let's just say the middle class is underrepresented when it comes to lobbying. It's one of the reasons people distrust Congress and no longer vote, which in turn gives special-interest groups more power in deciding who gets elected. It's a vicious two-edged sword that degrades democracy.

It's estimated nearly $10 billion will be spent on presidential and congressional elections in 2016. How crazy is that?

If raising money is critical to getting reelected, so is spending taxpayers' money to reward those who help get us reelected.

Political contributions have created an enormous number of future IOUs for both Republicans and Democrats. Screw the common good. We're the puppets of special interests, bankrupting the country to feather our nests and the nests of those who support us.

Some contributions are subtle. Donations to a member's nonprofit foundation. Funding a member's charitable pet project. Offsetting the costs of a member's portrait to adorn the committee room he or she has so faithfully served. It's all a bunch of bullshit to get around gift bans and limits on campaign contributions. Where there's a will, there's a way.

Just because something's technically legal doesn't mean it's morally right. Perceptions count, which is why no one trusts us to do the right thing anymore.

WE'RE NOT OBSESSED WITH THE TRUTH IN WASHINGTON

★　★　★

. . . but rather with well-meaning deceit and an adroit distortion of the facts. [*Laughs.*] If truth is telling it like it is, you've come to the wrong place.

Follow the leader. It all starts at the top and seeps on down. Remember those mythical WMDs in Iraq, and 'if you like your doctor you can keep your doctor.' Fraud and illusions have always been part of a successful politician's makeup.

Rationalizing lies is part of our DNA. It is what it isn't.

Even our government agencies have become Pinocchios. Misinformation is taken for granted. Prejudicial statistics, selectively chosen data, slanted surveys, purposeful omission of key facts, rigged numbers, outright lies. You just don't know who or what to believe anymore.

I'll tell you whatever you want to hear, and I'll do so with conviction and sincerity. In fact, I'd have to say I've learned to fake things pretty well.

Is it a lie if I truly believe what I'm saying? As far as I'm concerned, whatever viewpoint I embrace is the truth.

I see nothing inappropriate about embellishing the facts if it brings about a worthwhile piece of legislation.

Truth is hard to discern these days. By the time you think you've figured it out, the world has moved on to more pressing matters.

The secret to telling a successful lie is to repeat it ad nauseam until skeptics start wondering if maybe there's some truth to it.

Fact-checkers. Who cares? The public realized long ago that truth-telling isn't our coin of the realm. Our mendacious ways have become a cliché.

A case could be made this town's corruptive tendencies reflect our nation's declining ethical behavior. Cheating and lying have become the societal norm. So it's not surprising a lot of people no longer believe honesty's the best policy when it comes to getting what they want in life.

Voters select a congressperson based on their own bias and self-interest. In today's two-party polarized atmosphere, my half-truths and exaggerations don't really matter. What matters is that I'm a member of the political party that looks out for the interests and views of the majority of my constituents.

I've come to the conclusion the whole Washington scene represents a diminishment of civilization. Our country's in a free-fall to mediocrity, and Congress is leading the way.

HARRY REID'S A POMPOUS ASS

★   ★   ★

. . . sometimes a bit too clever for his own good. The same goes for McConnell and his pathetic lieutenants. Ditto for most of the House leadership bullies on both sides of the aisle. They wield too much dictatorial power, manipulating legislative procedures and denying members due process.

My constituents didn't elect the Speaker. I'm tired of being unable to vote or offer floor amendments on issues I feel are important. A democratic society thrives on open debate and free discussion. Not on laws written behind closed doors by the select few.

Committee chairs are always the biggest recipients of special-interest monies. That's why the key requisite to chair a committee depends on your ability to raise significant funds for a leadership PAC.

A lot of lobbyists are involved in writing legislation we pass in committee. Money talks. Yet my colleagues and I can't stop this regulatory cronyism without the consent of the House speaker and committee chairman. Needless to say, consent is seldom granted.

When you're the majority party, you want to stay that way. There's little to be gained by cooperating with the minority party. Why make them look good? Staying in power's the name of the game, even if the welfare of the country occasionally takes a backseat.

Surveys show the American people hate

Congress. But we know better. Incumbents still have better than a 90 percent chance of being reelected. That's because we've rigged the system—Republicans and Democrats alike—by redrawing district lines to heavily favor one party. In effect, we're selecting our voters. How's that for representation!

Gerrymandering's a nice scam that ensures members a relatively safe seat and easy victory. In a fair world, independent, nonpartisan commissions would be in charge of redistricting in every state. But why screw up a good thing? [*Laughs*].

The ongoing struggle for political advantage has created an antagonistic and vulgar environment, though it's fun to constantly snooker the Republicans.

Too much time's wasted on imaginative obstructionism designed by the party leadership. The manipulation of archaic rules and the creation of ludicrous loopholes have undermined the legislative process.

The budget process highlights our descent into folly. What a charade! We're supposed to pass a dozen spending bills every year. That hasn't happened once this century. How reckless is that?

You can't responsibly govern a nation with short-term continuing resolutions, backdoor spending, supplemental appropriations. And that doesn't include our annual orgy of Christmas tree riders filled with favors for special interests who understand the pay-for-play culture.

Seniority sucks. Most of the leaders in both parties—House and Senate—are living fossils who don't exactly convey an attractive and vigorous image of Congress.

We need to weed our geriatric landscape. Replace longtime careerists with new blood. People who understand the power of collaboration.

Members of the president's party see the president as their party leader and kowtow to his legislative demands. So much for the Constitution and the separation of powers. The breakdown's been going on for more than fifty years, and Congress is becoming irrelevant.

I FEEL
DISCONNECTED
FROM REALITY

★　★　★

. . . from the very people I was elected to serve. This town's like Oz. A cynical and cloistered place, far removed from life as I know it. Pull back the wizard's curtain and behold Congress in all its glory.

There seems to be a complete disintegration of confidence in government. A fear that government is its own special interest. That it can't do its job. That it makes mountains out of molehills. That it's presumptuous, wasteful, politicized, out of control, and doesn't give a damn about folks beyond the [Washington] Beltway.

We pass laws, then figure out ways to exempt ourselves from the effects of those laws. We do the same thing with tax policies. Rules don't apply to us, just the rubes we represent. And we wonder why they're pissed.

Once a bill passes in committee, I seldom see the final product or revisit the effects of its implementation. It's over and done with and time to move on to the next piece of legislation.

We seem to have an affinity for making fools of ourselves without recognizing our folly.

Everyone in Washington is out for himself. We all want more. And we're not the least bit embarrassed by our greed. It's just the way it is.

The average man on the street actually thinks he influences how I vote. Unless it's a hot-button issue, his thoughts are generally meaningless. I'll politely listen, but I follow the money.

Our party used to be a strong advocate for the working class. We still pretend to be, but we aren't. Large corporations and public unions grease the palms of those who have the power to determine legislative winners and losers.

I have to admit my job is better than most. A generous six-figure salary, another million-plus to cover staff and office perks. It's like owning your own business with someone else paying the bills. It doesn't matter if I support reckless spending and blow through budgets. Hell, once I'm open for business, other businesses give me money just to become my friend. [*Laughs*].

Like other members, I spend the majority of my time in the company of well-to-do donors, lobbyists, and other sophisticated folks. I'm comfortable in their world and often empathize with their views. Do they influence my votes more than the middle-class constituents I represent? Probably.

Most of my colleagues want to help the poor and disadvantaged. To a point. We certainly don't want to live among them. Or mingle with them, unless it's for a soup kitchen photo op. [*Laughs*]. Why do you think we wall ourselves off in residential enclaves with other well-educated elites? Poverty's a great concern as long as it's kept at a safe distance.

Average citizens are tired of seeing us wage wars that lack sensible objectives and exit strategies. Poverty programs that seem to perpetuate poverty. Paying farmers not to grow things. Education reforms that are as stupid as the students they're meant to help. Politicians sticking their noses where they don't belong.

There's a rising resentment and loss of faith between the American people and their government. They don't believe we really understand their problems. That things are just not right. That their children won't have the opportunities they had. They're scared. America's on an irreversible decline, and no one in Washington seems to care.

I'M A CLOSET MODERATE

★   ★   ★

. . . but damned if I'll reveal my true beliefs in these polarized times. Hell, I'd be viewed as a heretic by a majority of my constituents and colleagues.

The GOP have their crazy wingnuts, and we have our loony leftists. Screw them both. What we need are more common-sense lawmakers. Folks who see both sides of an issue. Who are open to accommodating each other's priorities. Today, both sides assume their views are the only logical ones.

I'm concerned my party has an activist far-left wing intolerant of center-leftists. Like the Republican Tea Party, these ideologues are much too rigid and extreme in their beliefs. And they're equally unappealing to mainstream Americans.

Extremists in both parties want all or nothing, and they want it now. They don't understand that a piece of the pie is better than no pie at all.

The key reason Congress is so dysfunctional is because moderates have taken a beating in the primaries. Ideological purists from both parties now occupy safe seats with harmonious constituencies. There's little incentive to move to the center and work together.

I'm tired of all the anger and rancor in today's political discourse. Each side has demonized the other, and the public good has suffered.

I've nothing against offshore drilling, but

I also want to see us invest in renewable energy. In our current hyper-partisan environment, you can't have it both ways.

As you know, I'm a strong advocate of improving our public schools. I also see the near-term value of vouchers and charter schools committed to lending a helping hand to disadvantaged kids. Especially inner-city kids. Hell, most of us send our children to private schools and wouldn't be caught dead sending them to public schools in places like DC. How hypocritical's that? It's time to set aside petty politics. Are both parties so fucking stubborn they can't work out a reasonable compromise on this common-sense issue? Our educational system's in the toilet, and all we do is snipe at each other.

I'm proud to be a Democrat assisting the poor, less fortunate souls in our society. That said, I occasionally wonder about my automatic 'yes' votes when it comes to funding various social welfare programs. Are these programs yielding the results we thought they would? They're certainly well-intentioned, though we don't do enough oversight and follow-through to see if things could be improved. Maybe it's time we find out what works, what doesn't, and why.

After decades of social spending, I have gnawing doubts about the power of the feds to always do the right thing. The government has a vital role to play, but that doesn't mean it always has to be a dominant role. Why do some of my righteous colleagues feel that's such a radical thought?

Look. Just as the GOP can't hope to survive as the party of no government, no taxes, no tolerance . . . we can't expect to survive as the party of government-dependent souls who simply want more for nothing. We need to temper our generosity, to be fiscally realistic, careful about piling up debt on our grandchildren and their children. When it comes to funding, we've got to take the future into consideration and stop thinking about just the here and now.

The inner me is a classic 1970s moderate. A true progressive when it comes to social issues, though I do feel Congress wastes too much of its valuable time dwelling on such concerns. On the other hand, I'm center-right when it comes to fiscal matters. I wish I had the guts to follow through on my beliefs, but I'd be toast in the next primary if I openly challenged my party's orthodoxy.

WE'RE TERRIBLE CUSTODIANS OF THE PEOPLE'S MONEY

★　★　★

. . . because we [Congress] don't have the willingness to conduct proper oversight of government agencies. Maybe if we didn't have to spend so much time raising campaign money, things would be different.

Fraud and waste are getting out of hand. Even the feds' morass of agencies and departments have no idea how to stop it. It's outrageous, but the public is inured to the incompetence. That's why I voice my anger in a press release, get credit for speaking out, and move on.

The most egregious cases cited by the GAO [Government Accountability Office] warrant committee hearings. Big deal. When testifying, agency heads just blather ambiguities and feel no obligation to be wholly truthful.

Look. Washington doles out more than $100 billion every year in erroneous payments under the Medicare, Medicaid, School Breakfast, and other programs. A $100 billion for god's sake!

It adds up. In the past decade more than a trillion dollars has been lost due to improper payments. Tally in uncollected taxes, delinquent debts, and the extent of the crisis is frightening. Is it any wonder people mistrust their government?

Just think if we had cut that waste in half. We'd have $500 billion to spend on repairing obsolete roads and bridges, or lending a helping hand to those in need.

I just don't know how much longer we can sustain this sort of rampant federal mismanagement, congressional gridlock, freewheeling debt, out-of-control entitlement programs, our aversion to taxes. Has our polarized form of government reached a tipping point when it comes to survivability?

The federal government's a sprawling mess. No one can possibly comprehend everything it's up to. Government agencies pretty much do what they want, viewing us elected legislators as little more than temporary nuisances. Here today, gone tomorrow.

With little congressional monitoring, regulatory agencies seem to operate on their own beliefs. Interpreting the laws we pass but never follow through to conclusion.

In a sensible world we would regularly revisit laws and regulations to see if they've had the intended consequences. Times change, and some may need to be fine-tuned or taken off the books. But who has the time?

The more laws we pass and fail to follow through on, the more common sense we seem to suck out of life.

THE NEWS MEDIA IS AS BIASED AS THE POLITICIANS IT COVERS

★   ★   ★

. . . even though it's supposed to be covering us in a nonpartisan way.

Journalists are a lot like the politicians they interview. The more elite ones are puffed up with self-importance and entitlement. And in their spare time they plot ways to achieve the fame and power they so rightfully deserve. [*Laughs*]. No surprise their favorite social event is the White House Correspondents' Dinner schmooze-fest. See and be seen. It's the name of the game.

Most people don't expect objective news coverage of election campaigns. Trustworthy icons like Walter Cronkite and Edward R. Murrow are artifacts of the past. Today, it's all about subtle headlines, nuanced camera angles, cunning editing and story placement.

Political columnists, TV commentators, and talk show hosts are inherently biased and aspire to effect election outcomes. Pretending otherwise is a thing of the past. You're either red or blue, and there's no in-between. Little wonder voters flock to TV stations, newspapers, and websites offering them the partisan news slant they believe in.

Politicians react to the opinions shaped by the media and polls. Think of the media as the Pied Piper, and we're the rats dutifully following their lead and developing our views accordingly.

Some of my constituents worship those talking heads on cable TV. They parrot their views to seem knowledgeable and hip. That's why I try to keep cozy with the chattering press, occasionally throwing 'off-the-record' breadcrumbs their way. It's all a game. Scratch me, I'll scratch you, and we'll both look good.

Cable news pundits have gained influential status in recent years, so it's always good to snag a live interview. The folks back home love it and consider me a celebrity whenever I appear on TV. God knows why.

The media cover Congress like a soap opera. They make something out of nothing. It's all about staging, storylines, trivialities, myth making, and myth taking. It's never about truth, the whole truth, and nothing but the truth. Straight reporting of the facts is too boring. The masses want to be entertained.

At election time the media loves to talk about a candidate's 'authenticity' and 'gravitas.' The public just wants someone they can relate to. Someone who'll give them what they want.

News and entertainment are one in the same. It's all a blur with theatre journalism masquerading as mainstream journalism.

I'M NOT HOPEFUL ABOUT THE FUTURE

★   ★   ★

. . . about Congress, about Washington. The political system's broken. And nobody knows what to do about it. People are too busy. Too self-absorbed. Too apathetic. Too stupid. Or maybe they've just plain given up on changing the status quo. I hear the anger, but it isn't being translated into momentous action.

Congress has created a culture of selfishness and corruption that's eroding the very concept of democracy. I fear things are so deeply ingrained we need an insurrection at the ballot box to right all the wrongs. To bring about any meaningful change in the way our country is governed.

I understand the lack of trust and resentment voters have in Congress' ability to do its job. But let's face it, there's no real incentive for us to change. Creative gerrymandering and the polarized electorate's propensity to vote the party line pretty much guarantees the reelection of incumbents.

In these politically divided times, people inherently vote for their party's incumbent during general elections for fear the opposing party's candidate will be too radical for their tastes. The only way to bring about real change is through the primary election process. It's a win-win for voters and the country. Vote out incumbents, yet still vote the party line.

What campaign promises should be demanded of these potential new members of Congress? How 'bout this? . .

They should agree to significant campaign finance reform without loopholes. Severely cap political contributions from individuals and PACs, and mandate full disclosure of all donors. Lobbyists should be prohibited from raising money for those they lobby. Compulsory, publicly financed primary and general election campaigns should also be on the table. It's time to show the American people Congress is not for sale.

They should agree to support independent, nonpartisan commissions to redraw congressional districts every ten years.

They should agree to overhaul obstructionist legislative procedures. Bring about a return to regular order in the House, especially when it comes to the budget process. Enough with the uncertainty caused by continuing resolutions. It's time to pass spending bills on time each year.

They should agree to limit the power of party leaders and abolish the seniority system. Why should the Speaker dole out committee assignments? And why should someone chair the same committee forever? It's time to rotate committee chairs every X number of years. To ban leadership PACs and fundraising quotas for committee chairs.

They should agree to cut back the number of committees and subcommittees so members can attend hearings and become more familiar with the issues at hand. Members also need to spend additional time in Washington doing their job. Recesses are fine, but let's have four-day Washington work weeks when Congress is in session.

They should agree to limit congressional service to X years, or set a mandatory retirement age of, say, seventy. We need a constant flow of new blood and invigorating new ideas.

I could go on, but you know what, it's all a damn pipe dream. Don't you see? Congress echos the excessive partisanship of voters. Everyone has such a loathing for the other party that meaningful change has no hope of evolving. Besides, you're lucky to get 20 percent of the electorate voting in primary elections. I fear those who govern and those who are governed will continue to watch out for their own self-interest.

God help us.

Lightning Source UK Ltd.
Milton Keynes UK
UKOW06f1459170616

276486UK00001BA/11/P